100 QUESTIONS about HOW THINGS WORK!

and all the answers too!

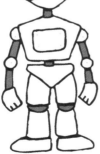

Written and Illustrated by
Simon Abbott

 PETER PAUPER PRESS, INC.
White Plains, New York

For John - who knows how most things work!

PETER PAUPER PRESS

In 1928, at the age of twenty-two, Peter Beilenson began printing books on a small press in the basement of his parents' home in Larchmont, New York. Peter—and later, his wife, Edna—sought to create fine books that sold at "prices even a pauper could afford."

Today, still family owned and operated, Peter Pauper Press continues to honor our founders' legacy of quality, value, and fun for big kids and small kids alike.

Designed by Heather Zschock

Published by Peter Pauper Press, Inc.
202 Mamaroneck Avenue
White Plains, New York 10601 USA

Published in the United Kingdom and Europe by Peter Pauper Press, Inc.
c/o White Pebble International
Unit 2, Plot 11 Terminus Rd.
Chichester, West Sussex PO19 8TX, UK

Library of Congress Cataloging-in-Publication Data

Names: Abbott, Simon, 1967- author.
Title: 100 questions about how things work! : and all the answers too! / written and illustrated by Simon Abbott.
Other titles: One hundred questions about how things work!
Description: White Plains, New York : Peter Pauper Press, Inc., [2021] | Series: 100 questions about... | Audience: Ages 7+. | Summary: "Children learn about how things in the world around them work through a series of questions and answers. Topics covered include household appliances, forms of transportation, architectural feats, medical devices, and more"-- Provided by publisher.
Identifiers: LCCN 2021016360 | ISBN 9781441336965 (hardcover)
Subjects: LCSH: Technology--Miscellanea--Juvenile literature. | Engineering--Miscellanea--Juvenile literature.
Classification: LCC T48 .A275 2021 | DDC 600--dc23
LC record available at https://lccn.loc.gov/2021016360

ISBN 978-1-4413-3696-5
Manufactured for Peter Pauper Press, Inc.
Printed in China

7 6 5 4 3 2 1

Visit us at www.peterpauper.com

Switch off the TV, turn down the radio,
and shut down the computer!
You're about to discover how things work!

Are you ready for a technological trip to
get the low-down on the gadgets and gizmos
that surround us?

Where does your soda can get recycled?

What happens when you flick a light switch?

How does an X-ray work?

Get ready for some dazzling data
and top techie tips. Let's go!

HOME SWEET HOME

Let's start in the place you know best! What amazing appliances can you spot at home?

Shall we head to the kitchen? (Don't stop for snacks!) How does a microwave heat your food so quickly?

Inside a microwave oven there is a gizmo called a magnetron. This gadget sends out a type of radio wave, which vibrates the food's water molecules at high speeds. When molecules rub against each other, they get hotter (think of how rubbing your arm makes it warm), and this movement then heats the food around it by conduction (a process in which things that are touching hot things also become hot).

Mmmm . . . I'd love some breakfast! How does my toaster work?

Inside every toaster is a set of coils that heat up as electricity passes through them. (You can even see this happening—they literally turn red-hot!) This heat caramelizes the surface of a slice of bread, or turns the sugars in the starchy bread slice into caramel. That's why toast tastes sweeter than bread!

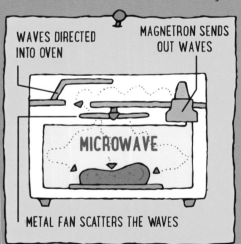

WAVES DIRECTED INTO OVEN

MAGNETRON SENDS OUT WAVES

MICROWAVE

METAL FAN SCATTERS THE WAVES

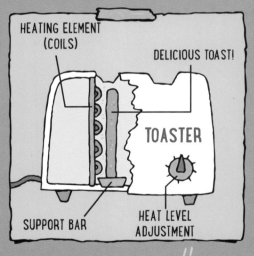

HEATING ELEMENT (COILS)

DELICIOUS TOAST!

TOASTER

SUPPORT BAR

HEAT LEVEL ADJUSTMENT

How do refrigerators keep my yogurt cool?

Inside every refrigerator is a series of coils, and in these coils is a substance called a refrigerant. How refrigerant moves from part to part is how refrigerators stay cool. Take a look!

Evaporator

The cold liquid absorbs the warmth from inside the refrigerator and keeps your food cold. The liquid converts into a chilly, low-pressure gas, and passes through the compressor to start the process again!

Expansion Valve

The liquid flows through this gizmo. The valve lets the liquid expand, which lowers its pressure. As its pressure lowers, the liquid turns into a gas. This process has a cooling effect because as a liquid evaporates, it draws heat out of its surroundings. (Think of how cool you get as you sweat!)

Condenser

The hot gas moves through these series of coils, called a condenser. As it moves, it quickly turns back into a liquid and releases heat.

Ventilation Fins

These direct heat through the back of the refrigerator and into your kitchen.

Compressor

It all starts here! Refrigerant enters the compressor as a gas. The compressor squeezes the refrigerant into a small space, which puts pressure on the gas. The increase in pressure raises its temperature.

The chores are done, and it's time for fun! How does a TV work?

Your TV is one part of a system that sends and receives moving pictures and sound. Way out in a TV studio, a camera records the visuals and the audio, then transforms the pictures into pixels and the sound into audio signals. These signals are then sent out by the TV station's transmitter and passed along until they reach your home. Your TV picks up this digital information, which includes instructions on how to turn it back into pictures and sound, and voilà! Your favorite show is on air!

How does my TV receive the signals?

Local TV stations use antennas to send signals as radio waves as far as they can. This is why you can't get your local TV stations everywhere: The antenna can only broadcast so far before the signal is lost!

Cable TV stations send their signals through underground cabling.

If you have a **satellite dish**, then you've got a souped-up version of an antenna! When a company beams TV signals via satellite, they convert their data into radio waves. These signals are beamed up into space, to satellites around 22,000 miles (37,000 km) above the Earth's surface. The satellites beam the signals back down to Earth, straight to your home's satellite dish.

So, I've got the signal, and switched on the TV! What happens next?

The signals your TV receives tell it how to arrange pixels (tiny colored dots of light) on its screen and what sounds to make every time something happens. Once it gets the picture (no pun intended), your TV becomes a giant picture flip book. Every second, your TV will flash different pictures to make it look like people are moving, or rockets are flying.

Let's head upstairs. How does my hair dryer work?

When you press the switch, a motor starts to spin the fan. This draws in air through the vents. The air absorbs heat when it passes over the wire heating element inside the hair dryer. Warm air makes water evaporate faster, so if warm air is blown over your wet hair, your hair becomes dry!

How does my bedroom stay warm?

That depends on what kind of heating system you have! If you live in an older home, you'll probably have a radiator, or a metal device attached to your wall. The pipes and radiators around your home are connected to a boiler. The boiler heats water, and a pump moves this water through the pipes to the radiators. It also sends hot water to the faucets around your home. (You can have a boiler, or a water heater, even if you don't have a radiator.)

Newer homes tend to have their rooms heated by gas, oil, or electricity. In these cases, a furnace heats air (either by burning fuel to do it, or by passing it over electric coils like a giant toaster), then pushes air through vents throughout your home.

How does my bedroom stay cool?

An air conditioner works in a similar way to a fridge, but rather than the food being kept cold and fresh, it's you!

Let's hop across to the bathroom. How does water come into a home?
The water from your faucet started out as rain, hail, or snow! This was collected in lakes, rivers, or underground sources, and was treated to remove anything harmful before it became safe to drink. Then it was piped into your home!

How is water treated?
There are three methods of water treatment:

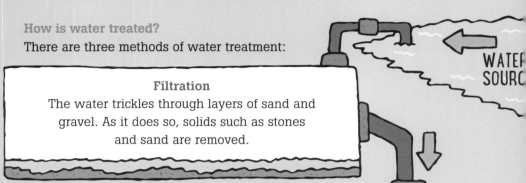

Filtration
The water trickles through layers of sand and gravel. As it does so, solids such as stones and sand are removed.

WATER SOURCE

Sedimentation
Water flows into a giant tank and sits there long enough for larger, heavier particles to settle at the bottom, before it's drawn into the next tank. Sometimes, chemicals are added to make tinier particles clump together.

Chlorination
Chlorine gas is added to the water to kill off microorganisms.

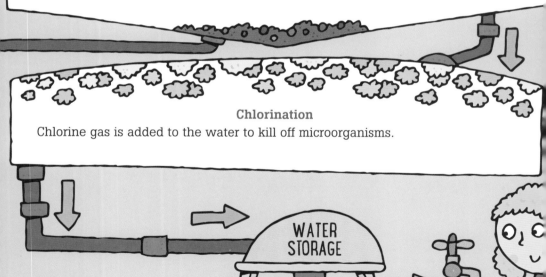

WATER STORAGE

How does water go from a treatment plant to my home?
If your family doesn't own its own well, then your water is stored in water towers, tanks, or reservoirs. Underground water lines (or mains) are used to carry this water to your house. From here, a water supply pipe will bring water into your home and out of your faucet!

How is wastewater taken away?

When you flush the toilet, the waste travels through a pipe to the sewage system. Before this waste is allowed back into the environment, it heads to a treatment plant where it goes through a thorough cleaning.

What processes take place in the treatment plant?

1. Large items such as diapers, wet wipes, bricks, bottles, and rags are removed. Special equipment is used to filter out grit and sand.

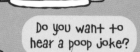

Do you want to hear a poop joke?

2. The wastewater is piped into settlement tanks where organic solid matter (that's poop!) sinks to the bottom and is pumped away.

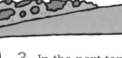

No! they always stink!

3. In the next tank, air is pumped into the water to create an environment for helpful bacteria to grow. These tiny organisms eat microscopic organic matter (flecks of waste, as well as some harmful bacteria), which allows the harmful stuff to clump together and form a sludge that stinks.

4. In this last tank, some of the sludge that was formed in step 3 is gathered up with the good bacteria and cycled back into the previous tank to be used again. Chlorine is added to kill off any remaining bad bacteria. This process also uses up the chlorine, so afterwards, the water can be released safely back into rivers and other water sources.

How does a busy city cope with its population's poop?

Let's take a look at New York City. With a little over 8 million inhabitants, the Big Apple's 14 wastewater treatment plants need to deal with around 1.3 billion gallons of wastewater every single day. To cope with this, the city pumps its poops through 7,400 miles (11,909 km) of sewer pipes.

I'VE GOT THE POWER!

Electricity is one of life's essentials. Let's get the low-down on this standout superpower!

How is our electricity generated?
There are many different methods. Take a look!

What are fossil fuels?
Long, long ago, plants and animals died in mud and were buried in the earth over time. However, they didn't form fossils like the ones you see at the museum. Instead, they decomposed under the weight and pressure of all the sediment and rock piling on top of them, and they turned into fuels we can burn for energy, such as oil, coal, and natural gas. These materials are burnt in power stations to release heat, which produces steam. This steam turns engines called turbines, which generate electricity. Some fossil fuels, especially natural gas, may also be used to heat your home, cook your food, and even power your AC!

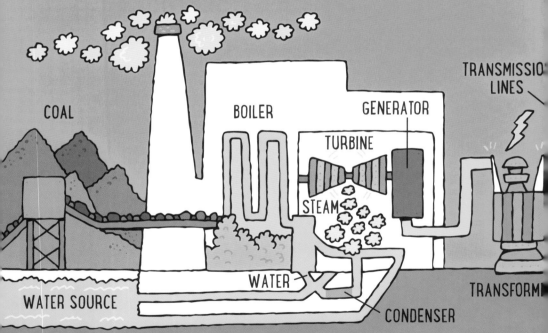

Why doesn't everyone use fossil fuels?
There are two major downsides to this method. First off, burning fossil fuels creates carbon dioxide gas. Carbon dioxide gathers in the atmosphere and is slow to break down when it gets there, so it creates a blanket that lets in heat from the sun but doesn't let it back out into space. This causes the Earth's surface temperature to rise, which can wreak all sorts of havoc with the environment. The other is that fossil fuels aren't renewable. That is, once you use it, you can't get more.

What is nuclear energy?

In nuclear power stations, energy is produced by a nuclear reaction, rather than a chemical reaction. To put it simply, we'll need to take a look at an **atom** first. Atoms, or basic building blocks of all things in the universe, are made up of protons, electrons, and neutrons. Every **element** (or type of atom) has a specific number of each of these things, but if you take away certain numbers of protons and neutrons, you can create entirely different elements. Because all atoms are also tiny bundles of energy, splitting an atom can also generate a lot of light, energy, and heat.

When we use nuclear power, we split uranium atoms into two smaller atoms. The heat this produces is used to boil water, and the steam spins turbines, which drives the generator and produces electricity.

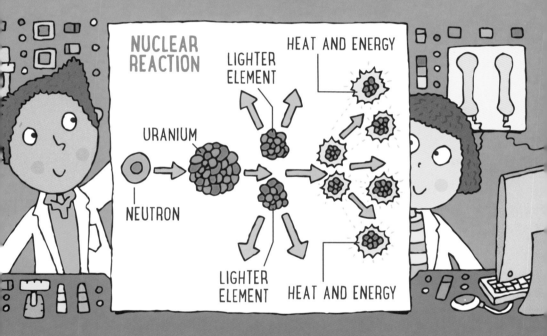

Does that mean nuclear energy is safer or better than fossil fuels?

Well, not completely. You wouldn't think it because it's so futuristic, but uranium is actually a naturally-occurring mineral in the earth. That means we can run out of it just like we can run out of fossil fuels. Also, the fuel itself is a hazard. Nuclear waste stays dangerously radioactive (meaning it can cause medical issues if you're exposed to a lot of it over long periods of time) for thousands of years, and an accident at a nuclear power plant can release tons of radioactive material into the surrounding area. In order to use nuclear power safely, you need state-of-the-art, well-maintained plants, highly trained workers, and places to store spent fuel safely.

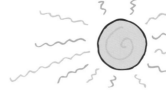

What are the alternative energy sources that can generate electricity and protect the planet?

Solar Energy

Sunlight is free and widely available. Inside every solar panel is a film of crystals. When sunlight hits these crystals, the electrons inside them get excited, which generates energy and, of course, electricity.

Wind Energy

Like sunlight, wind is unlimited. Wind energy turns the turbines' blades, which spins a shaft that drives a generator and makes electricity. This flows through a transmission, along power lines to a substation, then into your home or school.

Hydro Energy (Hydroelectric)

A dam or barrier is built to control the water flow from a river or reservoir. As water flows through channels in the dam, it drives a turbine and creates electricity.

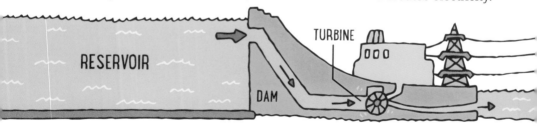

Tidal Energy

Tidal energy is a lot like hydro energy, but rather than dam a river, it uses generators built into bodies of water that feel the effects of the tides, including bays, estuaries, and the ocean itself. As the tide surges around the generator, waves turn its turbines, which produces electricity.

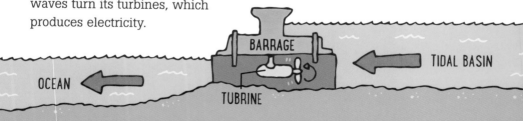

Geothermal Energy

This energy source uses hot water from inside the earth. Water or steam from reservoirs deep underground is brought to the surface via wells and pumps. Because these reservoirs exist close to underground sources of magma (liquid rock!), the water there is very hot and under a lot of pressure, so it produces a lot of steam as it's brought up to the cooler, lower pressure atmosphere above ground. This steam can be channeled into a power plant to turn turbines, which produce electricity. The cooled steam or water is then channeled into another pipe that takes it back down to the reservoir where it came from.

STEAM

TURBINE GENERATOR

COOLING TOWER

INJECTION WELL

HOT WATER

Biomass Energy

This method burns fast-growing plant material, corn, leftover wood, and paper and cardboard that can't be recycled. It can also harness the methane gas that is produced when garbage rots, and converts vegetable oils into biodiesel to heat our houses and power our vehicles. Just like fossil fuels, these collected materials are burned, and the resulting steam turns turbines. The upside to this method is that it can reduce waste, as we're taking trash and turning it into electricity. The downside is, like fossil fuels, burning biomass materials can produce dangerous levels of carbon dioxide.

FUEL
BURNING
GAS
STEAM
GENERATOR
TRANSMITTER
TURBINE

How does electricity get to my house?

Your electricity is produced in a **generating station**. These stations are connected by an electrical system, or power grid. The electrical charge travels through high voltage transmission lines to a **substation**. Here the voltage is lowered so that it's safe to be carried on smaller power lines. The electricity flows through distribution lines to your neighborhood. Small transformers on poles, or set in the ground, reduce the voltage again, so it's okay to use in your home!

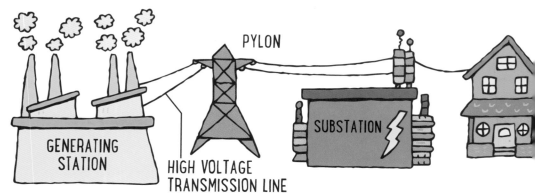

GENERATING STATION

HIGH VOLTAGE TRANSMISSION LINE

PYLON

SUBSTATION

Hooray! What happens next?

The power passes through a meter, then to a service panel. This is where breakers, or fuses, protect the household's wires from overloading. Finally, the electricity buzzes through wires inside the walls in a circuit of switches and outlets throughout your house.

REMEMBER! Electricity is dangerous, so take great care when you use any electrical appliance.

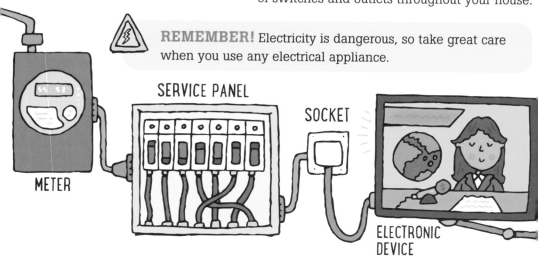

METER

SERVICE PANEL

SOCKET

ELECTRONIC DEVICE

What happens when I flick a light switch?

All electrical appliances, including a light switch, need a set of wires and components. This is called an **electrical circuit**. If the circuit is broken, then electricity can't flow. In the case of a light switch, if you click it one way, the circuit breaks, and the light turns off. Click it the other way, and . . . presto! You have light!

How does a light bulb work?

In incandescent *(in-can-DESS-ant)* light bulbs, there is a thin wire called the filament. When electricity runs through this wire, it causes the molecules that make up the filament to vibrate, which makes it grow hot and glow.

Is this how all light bulbs work?

Nope! Incandescent lights are an older style of bulb, but there are other types.

The first is the fluorescent *(floor-ESS-ent)* bulb, which contains gases that light up whenever electricity passes through them. Neon lights, which are another type, work the exact same way, only they use neon gas instead of the fluorescent's argon. Finally, LED (light-emitting diode) bulbs use a small crystal (a semiconductor) instead of a filament. When electricity strikes it, electrons inside it get excited and cause the crystal to light up.

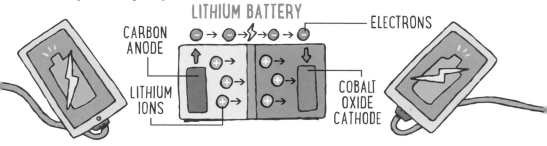

How does my tablet recharge?

Most tablets get their power from a battery, which can recharge by plugging the device into an electrical socket. Think of batteries as tiny power plants that rely on chemical reactions to generate electricity. They contain different chemicals that work together to move tiny particles called electrons around to make an electrical current. In a tablet or cell phone, the key chemical is lithium. When lithium passes through a network made by other chemicals from one end of the battery to the other, it gives off a charge that powers your device on. Plugging in your device resets this reaction and recharges the lithium in the battery.

WHAT A LOAD OF RUBBISH!

Do you throw your trash in the can, then forget about it? Time to get the low-down on your junk's journey!

How much trash do we need to get rid of?
In the U.S. alone, the average person generates around 4.9 lbs (2.2 kg) of garbage every day. The entire U.S. produces about 292.4 million tons of garbage in a year.

My trash is picked up on the curb side by the garbage truck. What happens next?
Your rubbish travels to the nearest licensed waste transfer station. Here the trash may be sorted into recyclables and other waste materials. Then your waste moves on to a recycling center, or to a landfill.

Which items can be reused?
Paper, cardboard, metal, plastic bottles, and glass can all be sent to be recycled. If they're in a good condition, furniture, bicycles, and books can be reused in second-hand stores.

How much trash is sent to landfill?
In the U.S., around 50%. Modern landfill sites are layered and drained to encourage the trash to decompose naturally, and to reduce the impact on the environment. Once the landfill is full, the waste is covered with a 2-foot (0.6 m) layer of soil and stone, which prevents debris from escaping and goes some way to contain pollutants.

Are recycling and landfill the only waste disposal alternatives?

Some of our waste is used to create energy, such as heat, electricity, or fuel.

Take a look at the methods that can be used:

Combustion

Trash is burnt in a contained chamber. The heat converts water into steam which drives a turbine and produces electricity.

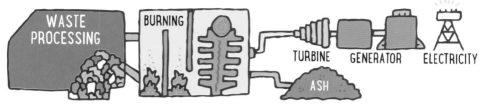

Gasification

This process converts materials that contain carbon into synthetic (manmade) gas. This can be burnt to produce electricity or developed further to make vehicle fuel.

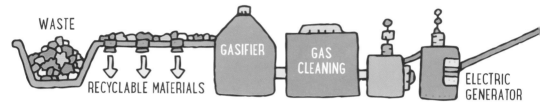

Pyrolization *(PIE-roh-lie-ZAY-shun)*

Trash is burnt at super-high temperatures in the absence of oxygen.

This makes synthetic gas and biofuel.

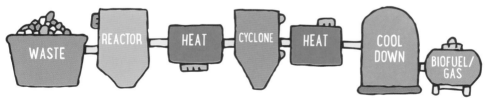

Anaerobic Digestion *(an-ay-ROH-bic)*

Bacteria breaks down animal or food waste to generate biogas.

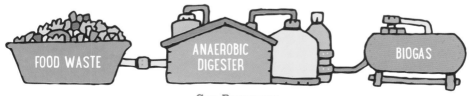

Gas Recovery

As landfill waste decomposes, a gas is produced. This gas contains methane, which is a valuable energy source.

Let's get the data on the top recyclables. How do these everyday items get reused? Take a look!

GLASS BOTTLES

How are these recycled?

Simple! The glass is sorted into colors, then washed, crushed, and melted. New bottles and jars are then molded into shape.

How many times can we reuse glass this way?

Glass doesn't deteriorate through this process, so it can be recycled over and over again, as many times as we need it!

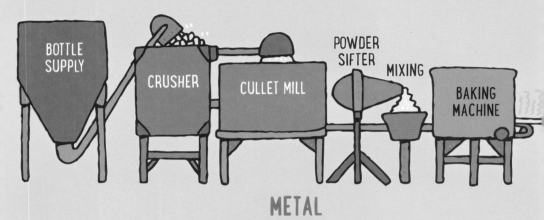

METAL

How is my soda can recycled?

Cans are sorted and cleaned, then melted to remove inks and lettering.
This molten aluminum metal is made into large blocks, called ingots.
These ingots are rolled into thin, flexible metal sheets and made
into cans, candy wrappers, foil trays, and more.

That's a lot of work for one new soda can!
Isn't it easier to make aluminum from scratch?

Recycling soda cans uses just 5% of the energy that's required to
create aluminum from bauxite, a sedimentary rock.

Why did the recycling can crusher quit his job?

It was soda pressing!

PLASTIC BOTTLES

Why should we recycle plastic bottles?

Plastic can take over 500 years to decompose, so it's important that we reuse plastic bottles, rather than pollute our planet.

How are the bottles recycled?

Some facilities can recycle around 2 billion bottles every year! The bottles are prewashed, and then a laser sorting machine separates the clear plastic from green plastic. A hot, soapy liquid then removes any labels and caps. The bottles are shredded, washed, dried, and heated to eliminate contamination.

What can this recycled plastic be used for?

Clothing, bags, car parts, furniture, paint pots, packaging, carpets, and much more can all be manufactured using recycled plastic. If it's reused as takeout boxes or soda bottles, the plastic must be sterilized and tested to see if it meets food-grade standards.

PAPER

You can't melt paper! How is this material recycled?

Paper is washed in a mix of water and chemical solution and turned into a pulp. This pulp is pushed through screens, then cleaned to remove staples, paper clips, glues, and inks. The resulting material is pressed through a number of rollers to create flat sheets, then dried and wound into a giant roll.

How big are these rolls?

Huge! They can be as wide as 30 feet (9 m), and weigh 20 tons. That's the same as three elephants!

TECH ACADEMY

Grab your gadgets and gizmos! Let's get the data on your everyday devices.

**First stop . . . the science lab!
How does a microscope work?**
Most microscopes contain two lenses, which are curved pieces of glass or plastic. These lenses bend rays of light and can make objects look bigger than they actually are. Take a look:

1

Light from the mirror is reflected through the object to the first lens. This is the first magnification.

2

This image is enlarged once more by the eyepiece lens, which acts like a magnifying glass.

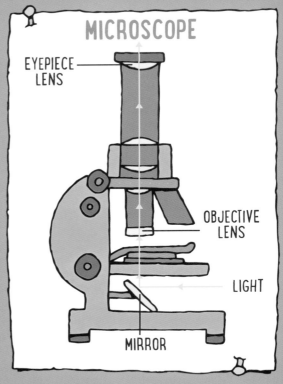

MICROSCOPE

EYEPIECE LENS

OBJECTIVE LENS

LIGHT

MIRROR

MAGNET

REPULSION   REPULSION

NORTH POLE

M A G N E T

MAGNETIC FIELD

SOUTH POLE

ATTRACTION   ATTRACTION

How does a magnet work?
A magnet produces an invisible force that pulls some metals toward it. The two ends of a magnet are called the north pole and the south pole. If you had two magnets, the ends that are the same would resist each other, and the ends that are different would attract each other.

Are all metals magnetic?
No. Only metals that contain iron, nickel, or cobalt.

How do compasses work?

Believe it or not, Earth has its own magnetic field, with magnetic poles at the top (north) and the bottom (south) of the globe. Compasses were invented over 2,000 years ago, when it was discovered that magnetized iron always points north. Sailors began to use early compasses to navigate the world's oceans and explore new territories.

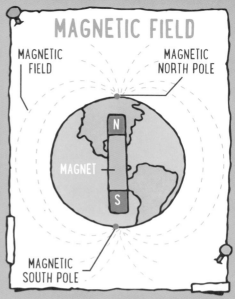

Now, onto a rather sticky subject. How does glue work?

Glue is made of polymers, which are large molecules and small molecules joined together. This makes the glue strong, flexible, and spreadable, and helps it stick to paper, wood, and plastic. Glue's vital ingredient is water. When you squeeze glue from a tube, the water gradually evaporates, leaving behind just the sticky polymers. In simple terms, the glue dries hard without water.
(You could've said that at the beginning!)

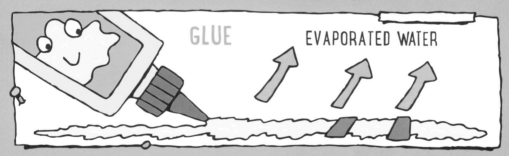

What happens when it all goes wrong? How does an eraser work?

As you write or sketch, graphite particles from the pencil tip rub off onto your paper. That's fine, until you make a mistake! An eraser is made up of rubber, a softener such as vegetable oil, and a scratchy material, or abrasive, such as pumice. When you rub your eraser over your pencil lines, the abrasive softly scratches the paper fibers, which loosens the graphite. The rubbing motion causes warmth, through friction, which helps the eraser become sticky and hold onto the graphite particles.

How long have erasers been around?

Edward Naime created the first rubber eraser in the 1770s. Before that, people used rough stones, and even rolled-up bread.

What are your hobbies or pastimes? Let's take a look at how some of the gadgets that make your hobbies work, work!

How does an electric guitar work?

When you pluck a guitar string with your fingers or a pick, the string vibrates. This vibration is sensed in the **magnetic pickup**, which is a bar magnet wrapped in about half a mile (0.8 km) of wire. This coil of wire sends a signal through a simple electric circuit, then through a lead to the amplifier. The amp takes the guitar's signal and boosts it through the speaker. We can hear the sound . . . let's rock!

Maybe a keyboard is more your style. How do digital pianos strike a chord?

Basically, a digital piano is a computer. When you press a key, it sends a message to the computer inside. Instead of typing out a letter, the key plays the sound of an acoustic (non-electronic) piano through the speakers. These sounds are called **samples**, and are created by sound engineers recording every single note of a top-quality acoustic piano.

How do cameras capture a moment?

A camera is a tightly sealed box that light can't enter. When you press a button, the shutter quickly opens and closes the aperture, which controls the light coming into the camera. The light that bounces off a person, object, or landscape passes into the camera through the lens, which focuses the light onto the camera's chemically-coated film. This film reacts to the light, changes colors, and records the image. Special chemicals are used to turn the film into paper prints of the image.

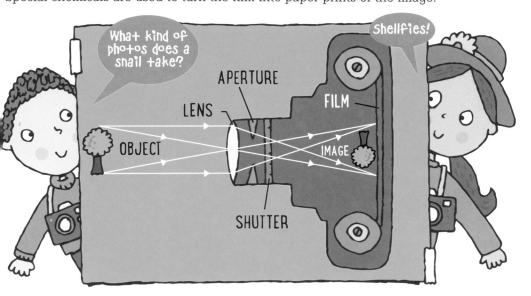

Does a digital camera work in the same way?

A digital camera captures an image using a special sensor instead of film, and stores the image on an electronic chip. The chip turns the image into electronic signals, which can be transferred to a computer. You can then view the image, email it, or print it out!

Are you one of the 4.6 billion people who use the internet? I'll take that as a yes! But how does all the world's knowledge get beamed into your house?

Let's get back to basics! What is the internet?

It's a global network of computers that are linked through various connections, including cable, fiber, and wireless signals.

When was the worldwide web created?

Tim Berners-Lee, an English scientist, invented the worldwide web in 1989. It's a collection of information pages (or web pages) that can be accessed on the internet. It's called a web as all the pages are linked.

How does the information I need get to my computer?

Let's imagine you're on a web page laughing at pictures of cowboy cats.
Here's how those images reach your computer:

1. Your computer sends a request to the web server that hosts your image.

2. The request is sent in a packet, or a virtual parcel that contains vital information, including the IP (Internet Protocol) address of the web server and IP address of your computer. These addresses make sure that the information is sent to the right place.

3. Special devices called routers and switches forward the packet from your computer to the web server.

4. The web server opens the packet and reads your computer's request, then directs packets containing the info you want (and directions on how to put it together) back to your computer, with the help of routers and switches.

5. Using the instructions in the packet, your computer pieces your image together. The information in the packets will contain your IP address and instructions so that your computer can put the image back together. Now you can see your cowboy cat!

This whole process can take less than a second!

I'm not sure which websites have the funniest cowboy cats.
How do I start looking?

Use a search engine! A search engine will browse its catalog of web pages for content that's related to your search. It makes this catalog using a program called a web crawler. This automated software scans the web and files away information about the pages it visits. When you type in your search subject, the search engine will give you the websites from its catalog that it thinks are the most useful, popular, and trustworthy.

How are websites created in the first place?
All computers follow a set of instructions, or codes. These are computer programs. These commands are written using a special language and specific rules, and they allow computers to perform a huge range of tasks.

WORLD IN MOTION!

Let's hit the road and get the low-down on planes, trains, and automobiles! Start your engines!

What's under the hood of a car?

If you're riding in a gas or diesel vehicle, you'll find an internal combustion engine under the hood. When fuel burns in the combustion chamber, energy is created. This energy moves the pistons up and down at great speed. The pistons' up and down motion moves the crankshaft, which turns the axle. The axle turns the wheels, and the car moves forward!

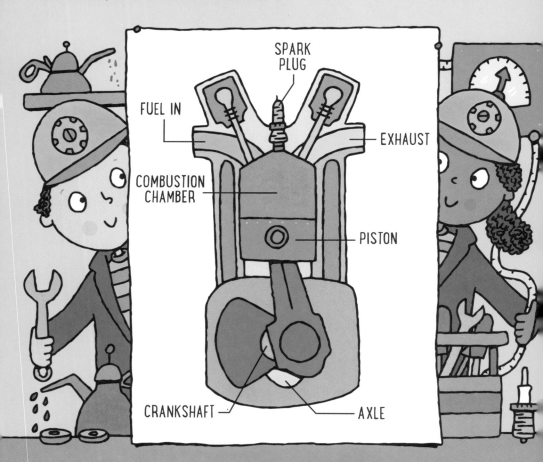

SPARK PLUG

FUEL IN

EXHAUST

COMBUSTION CHAMBER

PISTON

CRANKSHAFT

AXLE

Why does a car have gears?

The engine makes the crankshaft spin *very* fast. The wheels need to rotate more slowly, so gears are needed to reduce the speed of the spin. Gears help the car drive in different conditions, such as climbing a hill, or cruising down a flat road. The lower the gear, the slower the wheels turn.

How does an electric car work?

Rather than fill up with fuel at a gas station, these cars can be plugged into a charge point to store electricity in their rechargeable batteries. Power from this energy source is used to drive the electric traction motor, which turns the vehicle's wheels.

What might cars look like by the time I'm behind the wheel?

You might not be driving at all! Autonomous, or driverless, cars are expected to hit the road soon, once trial programs and safety checks have been completed. These cars will feature:

1. On-board cameras, radar, sensors, and light detection lasers that track the objects surrounding the vehicle.

2. Software that inputs this information, plots a route, and sends instructions to control the car's speed, steering, and braking.

3. In-car computers that are programmed with the rules of the road, and satellite navigation systems.

27

How does a helicopter fly?

A helicopter's wings are its rotating blades. The blades are curved on top and flat on the bottom, in a shape called an airfoil. Air flows faster over the top than the bottom, so there is less air pressure on the top of the blades. This causes the blades to move up and lift the helicopter.

How does a submarine move under the water?

When a submarine needs to dive, it fills up its ballast tanks (massive containers inside it) with water. This gives the submarine the weight it needs to sink under the waves. Propellers then push the vessel through the water. When the vessel wants to come up to the surface, the ballast tanks empty and fill with air. This makes the submarine light enough to float.

How do some passenger trains travel so fast?

These days, a lot of passenger trains are either diesel, electric (which is sometimes combined with diesel power), or magnetic. Diesel trains work a lot like cars in that they have engines powered by fuel. Electric trains are powered by either electrified third rails or overhead power lines. Finally, trains that run on magnetic levitation technology, or maglev, use a special track lined with magnetic loops, which work together with magnets set in the underside of the train. One set of these loops pushes the train forward, while the other sets repel the train just enough to keep it suspended above the track for a smooth and very quick ride.

How does something as heavy as a plane full of passengers get off the ground?
A plane has four elements that enable it to fly:

1 THRUST

Everything depends on a lot of air moving around the wings. So a plane's engine propels the aircraft forward at high speeds by pulling air into an intake and pushing it out with force from the other end. This is called **thrust**.

2 DRAG

Drag is the exact opposite of thrust. It's the force that resists movement forward. Drag will always push back every object in motion, including planes, so one of the most important keys to flying is finding ways to limit the amount of drag. Two ways to do this are to pull up the landing gear and adjust flaps on the wings to make the plane as small and compact as possible.

3 LIFT

Like helicopters, a plane's wings are curved on top and flat on the bottom. At high speeds (like those created by increasing thrust and decreasing drag), this design lets air flow up and over the wing faster than it can flow under, and this difference in speed creates a force that pushes up on the underside of the wing. This force is called **lift**, and it's how airplanes get airborne.

4 WEIGHT

Every object is pushed down to the ground by gravity, and this force is called **weight**. Weight is also the direct opposite of lift, so the two forces act against one another and keep a plane perfectly balanced in mid-air.

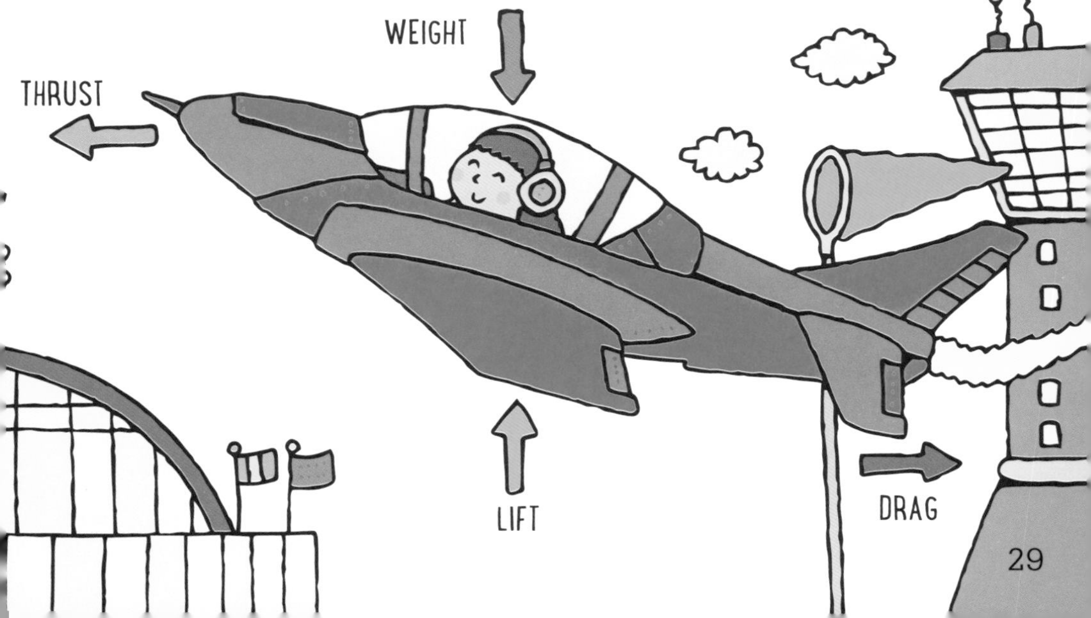

WEIGHT

THRUST

LIFT

DRAG

Hoverboards are super-cool! Shall we take a look at what's inside?

GYROSCOPES

Here's where the self-balancing technology takes place. The wheels send speed and tilt information to the gyroscope, which processes the data and sends it to the main logic board.

WHEELS AND MOTORS

Each wheel contains a motor, which allows the two wheels to move at different speeds and turn the board around.

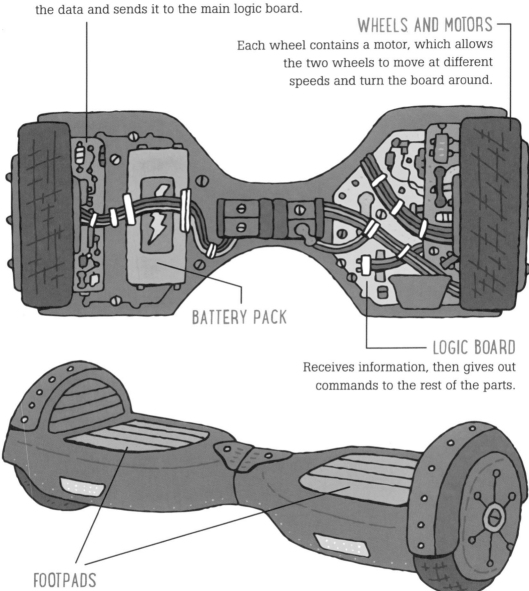

BATTERY PACK

LOGIC BOARD

Receives information, then gives out commands to the rest of the parts.

FOOTPADS

Each footpad has two switches: one at the front and one at the back. These switches give speed and direction commands to the wheels. Press down on the right front switch, and the right wheel turns forward. Activate the left back switch, and the left wheel turns backwards. This makes the board turn to the left.

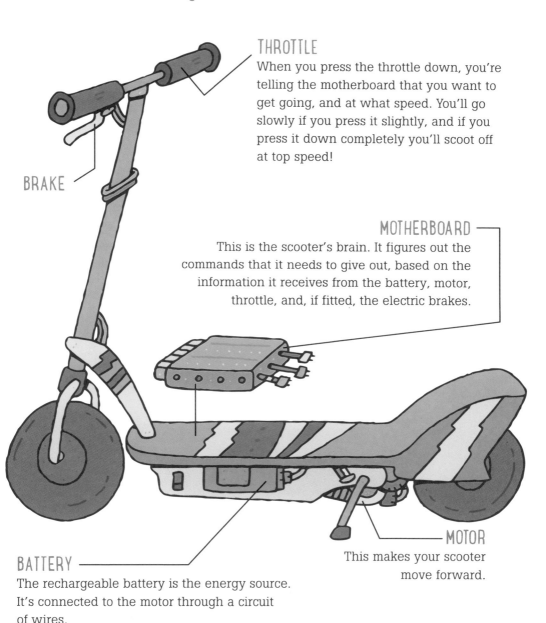

THROTTLE
When you press the throttle down, you're telling the motherboard that you want to get going, and at what speed. You'll go slowly if you press it slightly, and if you press it down completely you'll scoot off at top speed!

BRAKE

MOTHERBOARD
This is the scooter's brain. It figures out the commands that it needs to give out, based on the information it receives from the battery, motor, throttle, and, if fitted, the electric brakes.

MOTOR
This makes your scooter move forward.

BATTERY
The rechargeable battery is the energy source. It's connected to the motor through a circuit of wires.

So, I'm off! How far can I go?
It might take a while for you to achieve an electric scooter world record. The longest journey on this gizmo comes in at a staggering 6,267 miles (10,087 km). It took Song Jian of China 64 days, so you'd better pack some sandwiches too!

31

Now for a trip that's out of this world (literally). How does a space rocket get off the ground?

It's not an easy task, given the pull of Earth's gravity. The first thing you need to get into orbit is a LOT of fuel! At liftoff, a rocket uses up 11,000 lbs (4,990 kg) of fuel every single second. As this fuel burns and the rocket gets lighter, the gases blasting out of the rocket boosters thrust the rocket upwards. A rocket needs to travel at speeds of at least 25,000 mph (40,000 km/h) to leave Earth's gravity. This is called its escape velocity.

How can scientists operate robots in space when they're so far away?
Take the Mars rovers, which are a whopping 140 million miles (225 million km) from home. Because of the enormous distance between Earth and Mars, there is an average 20-minute time delay, so quick commands are impossible. At the beginning of each sol (a Martian day), the SUV-sized rovers receive a set of instructions, which they download via their antenna. The rover can then move to its target location, take pictures, and analyze rock samples. The rover is solar-powered, which means it doesn't need to be refueled—it just begins its day at sunrise with an on-board alarm. In the afternoon, after it transfers the data it's collected to antennae on Earth, NASA scientists plan the rover's tasks for the following sol. During the night, the rover must be kept warm, to protect its temperature-sensitive equipment.

The International Space Station has been orbiting the Earth for over 20 years. How does it stay in space?

To stay in orbit, an object has to travel at a constant speed around the Earth. With the International Space Station orbiting the Earth at a height of over 220 miles (350 km), it speeds along at around 17,500 miles (28,163 km) per hour. That's 30 times faster than a jumbo jet!

Can we circle back a little? What is an orbit?

It's a regular and repeating path that an object takes around a star, planet, or moon in space. The object, called a **satellite**, can be natural, like a planet, or man-made, like the International Space Station.

How do new arrivals dock at the International Space Station?

So, you're about to guide a 200,000 lb (99,790 kg) object traveling at 17,500 mph (28,163 km) toward the ISS. First, you'll need super-accurate hand-eye coordination. (If you're good at video games, this could be the job for you!) Astronauts use a laser gun to track their speed, and a computer makes the all-important calculations needed for lining the shuttle up with the space station. The docking vehicle slows down and glides into the station's air-locked docking port.

BRICK BY BRICK

Pop on your hard hat and grab your shovel! It's time to dig deep for some stone-cold statistics!

Let's start with the basics. How is a house built?

There are many different types of houses and construction materials, but the principles are the same:

1 Once the site has been cleared, straight trenches are dug and filled with cement. These are the foundations, which support the house, anchor it to the ground, and protect it from dampness in the earth.

2 A floor frame is constructed from timber.

3 Walls can be constructed from lumber or brick. Spaces are left for windows and doors.

4 Triangular frames are added to the top of the house which will support the roof. Frames for the internal walls are put in place, followed by the windows and doors.

What comes next?

5 It is important that the building becomes water-tight. The roof is covered with shingles and tiles.

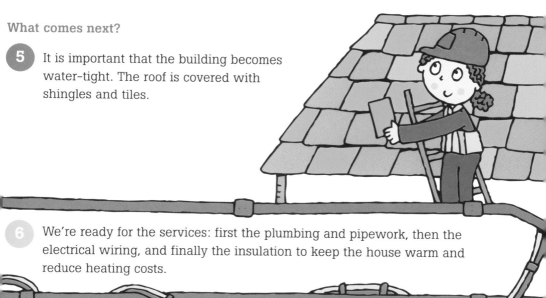

6 We're ready for the services: first the plumbing and pipework, then the electrical wiring, and finally the insulation to keep the house warm and reduce heating costs.

7 Plasterboard is added to the internal walls, then plastered and painted once it's dry.

WELCOME TO YOUR NEW HOME!

Let's take it up a notch! How are skyscrapers built?

Because of its weight, a skyscraper's entire structure relies on a steel skeleton called a **super structure,** which is anchored to a concrete foundation by a network of steel beams called the **grilling**. The super structure consists of horizontal steel beams criss-crossing the vertical beams sticking out of the grilling. All of these networks of steel beams and concrete point the building's weight into the ground in the same way planting your feet keeps you from moving. As for how construction workers get materials all the way from the ground floor up to the top, the answer is simple: They're lifted up there by crane!

MOTOR

CABLE

SHEAVE

RATCHET
SYSTEM

ELEVATOR
CAR

COUNTERWEIGHT

GUIDE
RAIL

Every skyscraper needs one thing: an elevator! How do they work?
An elevator is basically a pulley!
Take a look:

1 SHEAVE

A grooved pulley wheel which holds the cables (see below) in place. It's also a wheel that pulls the cable along a track, which is how an elevator car goes up and down.

2 MOTOR

When the motor is powered on, it rotates the sheave, pulling the elevator up and down.

3 CABLES

These thick steel ropes are what an elevator's car is attached to.

4 COUNTERWEIGHT

As the elevator goes up, the counterweight goes down. It weighs the same as a half-full elevator car, acts as a balance, and reduces the energy the motor needs.

5 GUIDE RAILS

These hold the elevator car and counterweight in place.

6 ELEVATOR CAR

You ride this!

7 RATCHET SYSTEM

Spring-loaded hooks which snap into the guide rails. This system stops the elevator car from falling all the way down a building if anything goes wrong!

Let's try and make sense of some complicated construction projects. How do you build a 26-mile (42 km) tunnel through a busy capital city?

Let's head to London and get to know the tunnel boring machine, or **TBM** for short. This amazing gizmo is the length of 14 London buses end-to-end, and weighs the same as 150 elephants! These metal cylinders have a rotating cutterhead to dig 20-foot (6.2 m) diameter tunnels. A conveyor belt behind the TBM takes earth out of the tunnel, and, as each section is cut, a 7-segment cement tube section is constructed to create the tunnel ring. The TBM has to weave its way through the existing subway network, sewers, cables, and underground rivers, so its **on-board laser guidance system** comes in very handy!

How are bridges constructed?

Let's take a look at how the world's tallest bridge, the cable stay Millau Viaduct in France, did it:

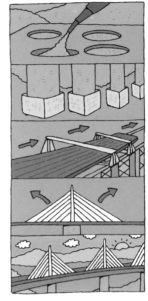

1. Dig 4 shafts for each **pylon** *(PIE-lawn)*, or tower that supports the bridge. Pour a thick concrete pad into each shaft for stability.

2. Add the pylons, which are towers of solid concrete.

3. Build the road deck next, separate from the bridge. Push the road deck onto the pylons, with the help of temporary towers.

4. This is a **cable stay bridge**, so you'll need masts! Lay these on the bridge, then join them together and hoist them into place on top of the pylons.

5. Fix the stays that connect the masts to the road deck, tension the bridge, and test the weight. Now you can remove the temporary towers.

Is this the way all bridges are built?

A cable stay bridge is just one example. Take a look at other options:

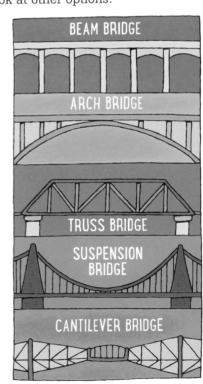

Beam Bridge
Horizontal beams are supported by vertical piers.

Arch Bridge
The load is distributed along the curved arch to the end supports. These bridges are very strong and stable.

Truss Bridge
A triangular framework of struts is built on vertical piers.

Suspension Bridge
The road deck is held in place by suspension cables. These cables are connected to 2 towers and anchored at both ends of the bridge.

Cantilever Bridge
A cantilever is a beam that only has a pier at one end, like a diving board. Two of these beams stretch toward each other to form a bridge.

How are dams built?

A dam is a barrier that blocks, or redirects, flowing water to create a reservoir. This can supply drinking water, irrigation for crops, and hydroelectric power. Here are a few of the most common dam types, plus how they work:

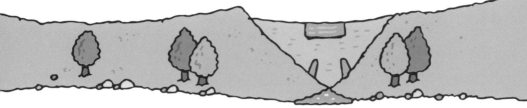

Arch Dam

These are usually built into rocky ravines with steep walls that can support the structure. They are built from concrete in an arch shape that curves upstream. This means that the water pressure is distributed evenly along the dam, making it secure.

Buttress Dam

These dams are used when the surrounding rock is too weak to provide a solid foundation. The structure is held in place by a number of solid concrete beams, or buttresses. The beams anchor the dam by adding weight and downward pressure.

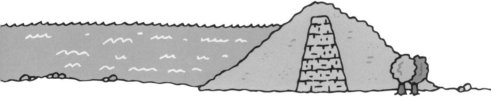

Embankment Dam

These hill-shaped dams are built from natural materials, and hold water back with their weight and sloped shape. There is a central core made from concrete or plastic, which stops water from seeping through.

Gravity Dam

These dams are built out of heavy concrete or masonry. Their sheer weight makes them super-stable, which stops the water behind them from shoving them over. These are great for narrow passages.

GET WELL SOON!

Let's take a trip to the medical center and find out what happens when our bodies go wrong! How do we get fixed?

How do glasses improve our eyesight?
We see an image when light is bent by the cornea (the membrane at the front of the eye) into the lens, which focuses light to the back of the eye onto the retina, which transfers signals to the optic nerve and then into the brain. Sometimes the cornea or lens focuses light into the wrong parts of your eye, making it harder for the retina or optic nerve to pick up signals. Glasses (and contact lenses!) work because they have curved, circular discs of glass or plastic that focus light where it needs to be.

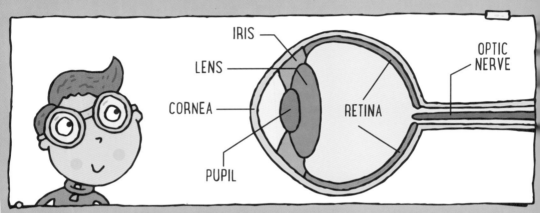

How does a hearing aid help someone with hearing difficulties?
Digital hearing aids are mini amplifiers!

1. A microphone receives a sound. A processor converts the sound into a digital signal.

2. The amplifier increases the strength of the signal that the user needs.

3. The speaker sends the amplified sound into the ear.

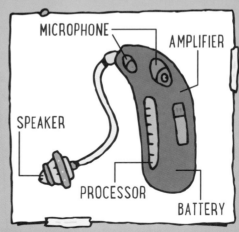

Some hearing aids work by vibration. They change the sound signal into a vibrating signal via a small pad that's held behind the ear. This allows sound to be sent directly into your hearing nerves, rather than through the outer and middle ear.

Why do doctors use a stethoscope?
A **stethoscope** has been a part of the medical tool kit for over 200 years.
It magnifies sounds, so helps a medic detect a heart murmur,
lung problems, or blockages in a patient's artery.

How does a doctor find out if my bone is broken?
First, you'll need to keep *really* still! A doctor can use **X-rays** to look into your body.
Rays of light pass through tissue and turn the film black. Bones block the X-rays
and leave white shadows on the image. A doctor will study the X-ray photo, then
figure out if your bone is broken.

What other gizmos and gadgets can snoop inside our bodies?

An **ultrasound** scanner sends high-pitched sound waves through your body, then picks up the echoes as they hit objects and bounce back. It measures these echoes to figure out what shape the object is, if it is solid or air-filled, and how deep in the body it is. A computer then converts this information into an image. Ultrasounds are often used to check the development of a baby in the mother's womb.

A **CT scan** rotates a series of X-ray beams around a patient. This gives the medical team a set of images of slices of the inside of the human body.

An **MRI scan** surrounds the patient with a super-strong magnet. This makes all the body's atomic particles, or protons, turn in the same direction. A radio pulse then taps the protons in certain areas into and out of line, which sends out radio signals to the scanner, and an image is formed.

Before a **PET scan**, the patient is injected with a dye that contains mildly radioactive (but perfectly safe!) tracers, or sugars that allow a doctor to detect certain types of cells. This lets doctors see how well certain organs and tissues are functioning. The tracers will collect in areas of high chemical activity, which might point to areas of disease, and these will show up as bright spots on the scan.

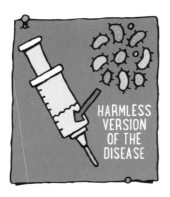
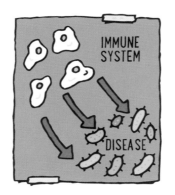
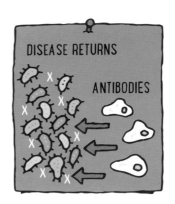

How do vaccines work?

1   A patient is given a small, harmless version of the disease.

2   A network of cells, tissues, and organs called your **immune system** makes **antibodies**, or tiny protein strands that help the body spot things that shouldn't be in it.

3   If the disease tries to invade your body again, you have the antibodies ready to flag it as an invader so your body can fight it off. In short: You're immune!

How do painkillers work?

Whenever you get hurt, your cells tell your body where you're injured by releasing a chemical called prostaglandin *(pros-tah-GLAN-din)*. Painkillers are chemicals that stop your cells from making prostaglandin, so your brain stops telling you you're in pain!

Some medical issues can get serious.

What happens during a surgical operation?

If a body part needs to be repaired or removed, then a doctor will have to open the patient up. An anesthetic will put a patient to sleep, or numb a specific body part. The surgery will take place in a super-clean operating theater, and the surgical team will have a huge selection of instruments at hand. Which instrument gets used will depend on what needs to be fixed. For small fixes, a laser beam might be used to seal the blood vessels as it cuts. A tiny camera called an endoscope can be inserted into the patient's body, allowing the medics to look at an injured body part. To avoid large cuts and speed up recovery time, a patient might be treated with keyhole surgery, or laparoscopy, which is when two small holes are made for the light, camera, and special surgical tools.

ESSENTIAL INVENTIONS

What are the gizmos that we can't live without? Let's check out these indispensable items!

How do my family's smartphones work?

A smartphone is a mini-radio that's always receiving signals from the antenna at your nearest cell tower or site. Most functions on a smartphone run on processors and computer chips, including internet browsing, image sharing, playing music, and gaming. The most important feature is the phone's operating system (OS). This lets your phone run multiple applications at one time, and can synchronize your data with other devices.

TOP HALF

BOTTOM HALF

CAMERA FLASH

CAMERA

SIM CARD

UPPER PART OF CIRCUIT BOARD

PROCESSOR CHIP

PLASTIC CIRCUIT BOARD PROTECTOR

INSIDE A SMARTPHONE

BATTERY

CHARGER/USB CONNECTOR

LOUDSPEAKER

MICROPHONE

HEADPHONE JACK

3D printers sound impressive. How do they work?

A 3D object is designed on a computer, which sends the information to the printer. The 3D printer melts a material such as plastic, rubber, or metal, then squeezes it through a nozzle onto a base, like icing out of a piping bag onto a cake. The 3D object is then built up layer by layer.

What objects can be built with a 3D printer?

Almost anything! You can print a guitar, a coffee cup, and even a bikini! Astronauts aboard the International Space Station have used one to make tools and materials, and engineers and doctors have been working together to develop custom artificial limbs for individual patients. Meanwhile, scientists are developing 3D bio-printers, which will create replacement body parts, such as livers and kidneys, using human cells instead of ink!

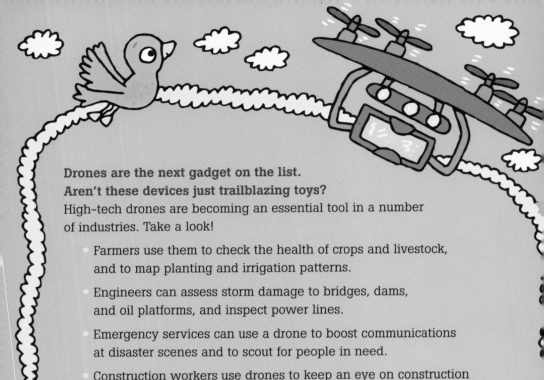

Drones are the next gadget on the list.
Aren't these devices just trailblazing toys?
High-tech drones are becoming an essential tool in a number
of industries. Take a look!

- Farmers use them to check the health of crops and livestock,
  and to map planting and irrigation patterns.

- Engineers can assess storm damage to bridges, dams,
  and oil platforms, and inspect power lines.

- Emergency services can use a drone to boost communications
  at disaster scenes and to scout for people in need.

- Construction workers use drones to keep an eye on construction
  sites, survey and map new pieces of land, inspect projects that
  are too long (like power lines and pipes) or tall (like bridges and
  high rises) for human eyes, examine sites and structures too
  dangerous for a human to enter, and more.

How do drones fly?

Drones are usually controlled by a smartphone or tablet, with apps that can
program flight paths, control a drone's every movement, and monitor their
batteries. As for how a drone flies, they're miniature helicopters, only with
four sets of rotors. Two of these rotors spin clockwise, and the other two move
counterclockwise. Together, these rotors keep the drone balanced,
and through each rotor, a pilot can control where the drone goes.

Let's take a trip to the store! How do bar code scanners work?

On the back of every product, there's a little white rectangle with black lines. This is called the **bar code**. Think of it as an on and off switch. The black lines mean on, while the white spaces between them mean off.

- When the scanner shines an LED or laser light onto this bar code, light is either absorbed by the black stripes or reflected by the white spaces onto a light-detecting piece called the **photoelectronic cell**.

- The cell then takes a look at all the ons and offs in sequence, puts them together as binary code (a computer's "language," where on $= 1$ and off $= 0$), and translates the code into text.

- This text is sent to the store's computer database, which pulls up information about the product, including its price, maker, and how many the store has sold.

All of this happens the second you hear a beep!

How do robots work?

The majority of robots are made up of the following components:

- A motor
- A sensor system
- A power supply
- A computer "brain" that controls the elements above

Special scientists called **roboticists** create computer programs and sensor systems to help robots navigate, see obstacles, and recognize images. Built-in microphones and small sensors can increase a robot's ability to figure out its environment.

A roboticist sounds like a super-cool job. How can I build great gadgets and gizmos in the future?

Anyone can become an inventor. It's your ideas and imagination that matter most! You need to be able to identify gaps in human knowledge, problems that need a solution, or existing gadgets that could be improved. With the technology that's available to you, it's never been easier to sketch ideas, make simple prototypes, test your gizmo, share demos, and get feedback from your friends and family.

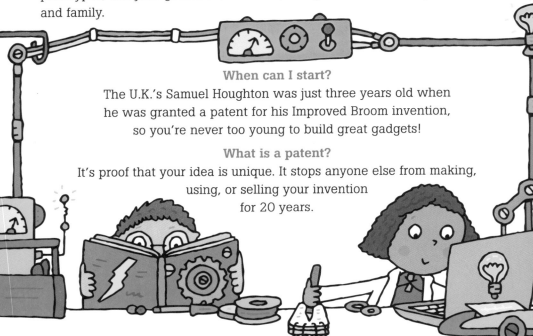

When can I start?

The U.K.'s Samuel Houghton was just three years old when he was granted a patent for his Improved Broom invention, so you're never too young to build great gadgets!

What is a patent?

It's proof that your idea is unique. It stops anyone else from making, using, or selling your invention for 20 years.

Let's open up the ideas factory! What could technology look like in the future?

- Bricks that could store energy and help heat our houses
- Robotic guide dogs to support people who are visually impaired
- "Living" robots that could collect microplastics from our oceans
- Labels or packaging that could change color when food decays
- Tiered floating farms that could grow fruit and vegetables in nutrient-rich liquid rather than soil
- Anything else you can think of!

It's good to remember that groundbreaking inventions aren't always welcomed right away. When Thomas Edison invented the electric light bulb over 150 years ago, the British Parliament told him that his invention was "unworthy of the attention of practical or scientific men."

So be patient. Be determined. And dream big!

CHECK OUT ALL OF THE FANTASTIC FACTS IN THIS SENSATIONAL SERIES!

100 Questions about the
Amazon Rainforest

100 Questions about Bugs

100 Questions about Cats

100 Questions about Colonial America

100 Questions about Dinosaurs

100 Questions about Dogs

100 Questions about Extreme Weather

100 Questions about How Things Work

100 Questions about the Human Body

100 Questions about Oceans

100 Questions about Outer Space

100 Questions about Pirates

100 Questions about Rocks & Minerals

100 Questions about Sharks

100 Questions about Spies

100 Questions about Women Who Dared